THE ELEMENTS

Sodium

Anne O'Daly

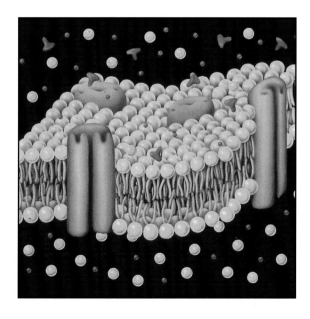

BENCHMARK BOOKS

New Hanover County Public Library
201 Chestnut Street
Wilmington, NC 28401

Benchmark Books
Marshall Cavendish Corporation
99 White Plains Road
Tarrytown, New York 10591

Library of Congress Cataloging-in-Publication Data
O'Daly, Anne, 1966–
Sodium / Anne O'Daly.
p.   cm. — (The elements)
Includes index.
ISBN 0-7614-1271-9
1. Sodium—Juvenile literature. [1. Sodium.] I. Title.
II. Elements (Benchmark Books)
QD181.N2 03 2001
546'.382—dc21   2001025253

Printed in Hong Kong

Picture credits
Front cover: Corbis/Patrick Bennett.
Back cover: Image Bank/Chris Close.
AKG London: 16.
Corbis: Amos Nachoum 26; Gianni Dagli Orti 10; José Manuel Sanchis Calvete 9;
Layne Kennedy 20; Patrick Bennett 23; Ted Streshinsky 30.
Image Bank: Antony Edwards 5; Chris Close 22; Macduff Everton 4; Steve Allen 18 (left).
Pilkington plc: 18 (right).
Science Photo Library: Andrew McClenaghan 7; Charles D. Winters 15;
Francis Leroy/Biocosmos i, 25; Martyn F. Chillmaid 6; Maximilian Stock Ltd iii, 12.
Still Pictures: Klaus Andrews 24; Somboon-Unep 17.
Travel Ink: Nigel Bowen-Morris 8.
TRIP: A. Lambert 13, 14; Spencer Grant 27.

Series created by Brown Partworks Ltd.
Designed by Sarah Williams

Contents

What is sodium?

The oceans get their saltiness from dissolved sodium chloride crystals, which are made up of sodium and chlorine atoms bound together in regular patterns.

When you sprinkle salt on your food, wash with soap, or bake a cake, you are using sodium. Sodium is a metal, but you are unlikely to find it on its own. It is so reactive that it almost always exists joined to other elements, in compounds.

Inside the sodium atom

The secret as to why sodium is so reactive lies inside its atoms. Atoms are the tiny building blocks that make up all the chemical elements. Inside each atom are even smaller particles: protons, neutrons, and electrons. Protons have a positive electrical charge and are found in the nucleus at the center of the atom. Neutrons have no electrical charge. They cluster with the protons inside the nucleus. Electrons revolve around the nucleus in a series of shells.

The number of protons inside an atom gives each element its atomic number. Sodium has an atomic number of 11, which tells us there are 11 protons in the nucleus. The protons and electrons are in balance, so sodium atoms also contain 11 electrons. The electrons are held in three electron

SODIUM ATOM

Nucleus | First shell
Second shell
Third shell

The sodium atom contains 11 electrons, which spin around the nucleus in three electron shells. There are two electrons in the first shell, eight in the second shell, and one in the third shell.

DID YOU KNOW?

WHAT'S IN A NAME?

Sodium gets its name from soda, a compound that contains it. Compounds of sodium were known about and used long before anyone had discovered the element. The element's chemical symbol is Na, from its Latin name, *Natrium*.

Trying to be stable

Atoms are most stable if their outermost electron shell is full. Some atoms share electrons with other elements to make them stable. For sodium, however, the easiest way to get a stable arrangement of electrons is to lose the single electron in the third electron shell. This outer electron is transferred to other elements in chemical reactions, and the transfer forms a chemical bond with the other element. Sodium loses its outermost electron easily, so sodium is a highly reactive element.

shells, with two electrons in the first shell, eight in the second, and one in the third shell. The nucleus of most sodium atoms contains 12 neutrons. The protons and neutrons combine to give sodium an atomic mass of 23.

Sodium belongs to Group I of the periodic table, along with metals such as rubidium and potassium.

Sodium atoms in a vapor are responsible for giving these superhighway lights their orange glow.

Special characteristics

A piece of freshly cut sodium is bright and shiny with a silvery sheen. It does not stay bright for long, however. The cut surface tarnishes within minutes, as the sodium reacts with oxygen from the air to form a dull layer of sodium oxide. Because of this, sodium has to be stored under oil or in an atmosphere of nitrogen gas.

Sodium is a metal, and it shares certain characteristics with other metals. In metallic elements, the electrons in the outer shell are not held tightly by their atoms. They are free to move around the whole element in a kind of electron "sea." This moving sea of electrons can carry heat and electricity,

Like other metals in Group I of the periodic table, sodium is very soft. This block of sodium metal has been recently cut with a knife, and you can see that the cut surface (on the left) is still relatively shiny, because it has not had time to react with the air.

so metals are generally good conductors of both. Sodium is such a good conductor of electricity that some people have suggested using it in place of copper in electrical wires.

Soft and light

You probably think of metals as being hard and tough, but sodium is soft enough to cut with a knife. It is light, too, with a density of 0.97 grams per cubic centimeter. Density is a measure of the

THE FLAME TEST

Sodium burns with a bright orange flame. All the Group I metals burn with a distinctive color. Scientists can use this as a test for the metal. They take a piece of platinum wire and moisten it with hydrochloric acid. Then they dip the end of the wire into the substance being tested and hold it in a flame. This is called a flame test. The other Group I metals show different colors. Lithium burns with a scarlet flame, and potassium with a lilac flame. Rubidium produces a red flame, and cesium burns with a blue flame.

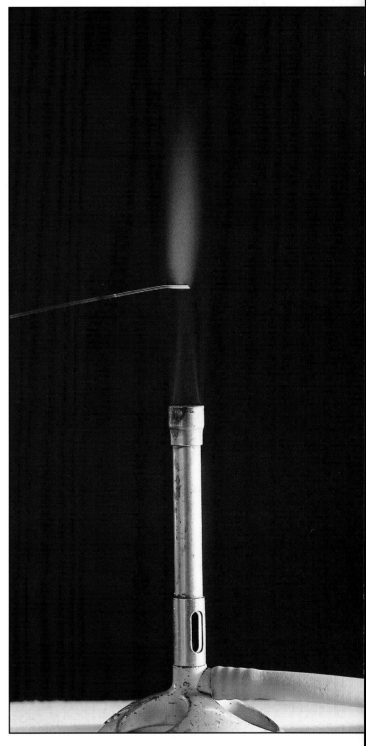

amount of matter a substance has in a given volume. Sodium has a low density because its atoms are fairly big, and the amount of material each atom contains is spread out in a relatively large volume. Sodium is light enough to float on water.

Melting and boiling

Sodium has a relatively low melting point. It melts (turns to liquid) when it is heated to just 206.6°F (97°C), which is below the boiling point of water (212°F, or 100°C). Sodium has a low melting point because the attraction between the atoms and the moving sea of electrons is quite weak. This means that it does not take much energy to make the metal melt. However, sodium has a high boiling point. The element boils (forms a vapor) when it is heated to a roasting 1,638°F (892°C).

Sodium burns with a yellowish orange flame in the flame test. This happens when the heat excites the atoms so that they emit energy in the form of light.

Where sodium is found

Scientists have found sodium traces in meteorites—chunks of rock that fall to Earth from space. This meteorite, which landed near Grootfontein in Namibia, South Africa, is the largest in the world.

Most of the elements are formed in the stars. Hydrogen, the lightest and most simple of all the elements, first appeared during the Big Bang, right at the beginning of the Universe. Now, in stars such as our Sun, hydrogen atoms are joined together to make helium, the next lightest element. After the supply of hydrogen is used up, helium atoms join together, and beryllium, carbon, and oxygen are created. In massive stars—at least four times heavier than our Sun—there will be enough heat and energy to make even heavier elements, including sodium. Astronomers can still see evidence

of sodium that was produced by earlier generations of stars in the Universe. For example, sodium exists in the outer atmosphere of the Sun and other stars.

Abundant sodium

Sodium is relatively common on Earth. It is the most common of all the elements in Group I of the periodic table, and it is the fourth most abundant element on the planet, making up 2.6 percent of Earth's crust. In nature, sodium joins up with other elements to form a wide range of compounds. By far the most common sodium compound is sodium chloride, or common salt.

If you have ever swallowed a mouthful of seawater you will know that the sea contains salt. Seawater contains about 3 percent dissolved sodium chloride— a supply that will never run out. On land, sodium chloride is found as the mineral halite, which is also called rock salt. Halite is dissolved in the water of some inland lakes, such as the Great Salt Lake in Utah. If the inland lake dries up, the water evaporates into the atmosphere, leaving the salt behind.

Halite also exists in deep underground deposits. These deposits originally formed as salt beds in ancient oceans that have long since dried up. The salt became buried deep under layers of sediment, which pressed the salt crystals together to form hard rock. In some places— such as Texas and Louisiana—the salt has been pushed up through the ground to the surface, where it forms arched structures called salt domes.

Impurities in this halite crystal show up as pinkish purple. Pure halite has no color and is completely transparent.

Halite mining

Halite is mined commercially, because it is an important source of sodium chloride. Sodium chloride is useful by itself and as a source of the individual elements sodium and chlorine. It is also the main starting point for many other valuable sodium compounds, including sodium hydroxide and sodium carbonate. There are important halite deposits in many parts of the world, including Salzburg in Austria, Stassfurt in Germany, and Galicia in Poland and Ukraine. The United States is the world's largest producer of salt. There are massive underground deposits in Kansas, Louisiana, Michigan, New York, Ohio, Oklahoma, and Texas.

As well as being found in halite, sodium occurs in many other minerals, including sodium nitrate (Chile saltpeter), cryolite, amphibole, and zeolite. It is also present in feldspar crystals in granite and in volcanic rocks.

How sodium was discovered

People have known about sodium compounds for thousands of years. The ancient Egyptians used soda, which they called natron, for preserving dead bodies for burial. Sodium carbonate—also called soda ash or neter—is written about in the Old Testament of the Bible. It was made by burning plants and then taking the compound from the ashes.

Davy's electricity

The element sodium was first isolated by English scientist Sir Humphry Davy (1778–1829). In about 1800, Davy became interested in studying the chemical effects of electricity. He decided that the best way to make certain chemical compounds decompose (fall apart) would be to pass an electric current through them.

In 1807, Davy used this method with a sample of potash (potassium carbonate) and managed to separate out the metal potassium. A few days later, he isolated sodium by passing a current through common salt (sodium chloride). The technique that Davy used was later called electrolysis. Davy used electrolysis to isolate other elements, and in 1808 he discovered calcium, strontium, barium, and magnesium.

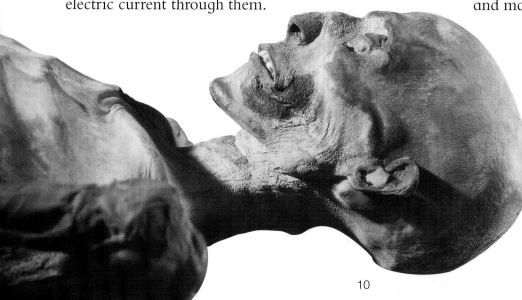

In ancient Egypt, mummification took up to 70 hours and involved covering the dead body with natron (soda) to dry it out completely.

How sodium is extracted

Today, sodium is extracted using electrolysis, the same process that Humphry Davy used to isolate the element nearly 200 years ago. Electrolysis is particularly useful for breaking down compounds that are too stable to break apart through chemical reactions or by heating them. Electrolysis needs two electrodes—one positive and one negative—and an electrolyte (a substance that will transmit electricity).

Using a Down's cell

The starting point for extracting sodium is sodium chloride, or common salt. It is melted and placed in a Down's cell. This is a cylindrical steel cell that contains two electrodes. The positive electrode, called the anode, is a rod made out of graphite (a type of carbon). The negative electrode, called the cathode, is a ring of steel that goes around the anode. The electrolyte is the molten sodium chloride.

When sodium chloride is melted, the sodium ions and the chloride ions are free to move around. The positively charged sodium ions are attracted toward the negatively charged steel electrode. The chloride ions are negatively charged

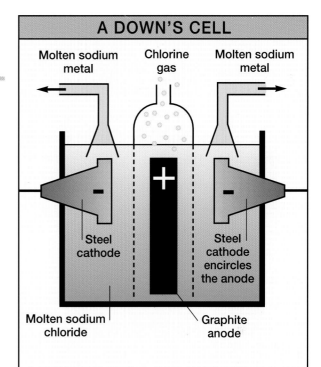

A DOWN'S CELL

Molten sodium metal — Chlorine gas — Molten sodium metal

Steel cathode

Steel cathode encircles the anode

Molten sodium chloride

Graphite anode

A Down's cell is used in the electrolysis of sodium chloride, to extract sodium metal and chlorine gas. The dashed lines around the anode represent a steel gauze that keeps the sodium and chlorine separate and prevents them from reforming sodium chloride.

and move to the positive graphite electrode. It is very hot inside the Down's cell, so the sodium (which has a low melting point) turns into molten sodium metal. This metal is so light that it floats to the top of the cell, where it can be drained off.

Chlorine is also formed in a Down's cell during the process of electrolysis, and gas molecules (Cl_2) bubble up to the surface. A steel gauze separates the sodium and the chlorine to stop them reacting and turning back into sodium chloride.

How sodium reacts

Chlorine is a deadly poisonous gas. Sodium is so reactive that it has to be stored under oil. When these two elements come together, they make sodium chloride—common table salt. Why should two such reactive elements form such a harmless and stable compound?

Sharing electrons

As we have seen, each sodium atom has 11 electrons arranged in a series of three shells. The two inner shells contain two and eight electrons. These shells are full, so they are stable. The outer electron orbits the nucleus all by itself. To get a stable arrangement of electrons, the atom needs to lose this lone electron. The single electron is easily lost because it is shielded from the attractive pull of the protons in the nucleus by the inner electrons.

Chlorine has 17 electrons, also arranged in three shells. The first two electron shells contain two and eight electrons, which are stable arrangements. The outer shell contains seven electrons.

There are many types of salt, or sodium chloride. Rock salt and sea salt have very large crystals, while table salt and popcorn salt have very small crystals.

When sodium metal is heated and placed in chlorine, it burns with a bright yellow flame. At the same time, tiny particles of sodium chloride are formed.

A sodium atom has to lose its single outer electron to get a stable arrangement. A chlorine atom needs to gain an electron to become stable. When sodium and chlorine are mixed together, the sodium loses its outer electron to the chlorine atom and becomes a positively charged ion (Na^+). The chlorine atom becomes a negatively charged ion (Cl^-). Both ions have a more stable electron arrangement than the atoms from which they formed. As long as the two ions stay together, they are unlikely to react with anything else.

ATOMS AT WORK

A sodium atom has 11 electrons arranged in three shells around the nucleus. The outer shell contains just one electron. The atom needs to lose this electron to get a stable arrangement.

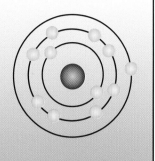

A chlorine atom has 17 electrons arranged in three shells. The outer shell contains seven electrons. The atom needs to gain an extra electron to get a stable arrangement.

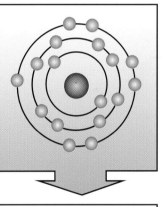

The lone outer sodium electron is transferred to the chlorine atom, making a sodium ion and a chlorine ion. The ions have filled outer shells and are more stable than the atoms.

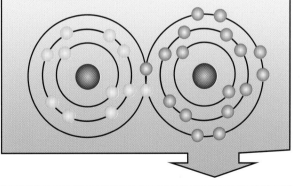

The transfer of the electron forms a chemical bond that holds the atoms together. The reaction that takes place can be written like this:

Na + Cl → NaCl

Like charges attract and unlike charges repel (push each other away). The attraction between the positive sodium ion and the negative chlorine atom holds the ions together in a chemical bond. This type of bond is called ionic.

Ionic compounds

Sodium reacts with other nonmetals to produce ionic compounds. Ionic compounds are generally solids at room temperature. They also have high melting and boiling points, because the attraction between the ions is so strong that it takes a lot of heat to pull them apart. Ionic compounds dissolve in water but not in organic (carbon-containing) solvents. When they are melted or dissolved in water, they separate into their ions. The ions are free to move around and will conduct electricity if an electric current is passed through the substance.

Sodium metal burns brightly when it is heated in oxygen, as it does in chlorine. When metals react with oxygen, they form products called oxides.

Reactions with oxygen

When a piece of sodium is exposed to air, it reacts with oxygen to make sodium oxide (Na_2O). If there is plenty of oxygen, the sodium and oxygen react to give sodium peroxide. This is a yellowish white solid with the chemical formula Na_2O_2. It is used as a bleach because it reacts with many colored compounds to give white products. The peroxide can also be made by reacting sodium oxide with oxygen.

Under special conditions, when the pressure of oxygen is very high, sodium and oxygen will react together to make sodium superoxide (NaO_2).

Other reactions

When it is heated to above 572°F (300°C), sodium reacts with hydrogen to give sodium hydride (NaH). It also reacts with sulfur to make sodium sulfide (Na_2S) in an energetic reaction. Sodium can react with

14

carbon in two different ways. It can form the ionic compound sodium carbide (Na_2C_2), which contains the C_2^{2-} ion. It can also form a number of compounds with graphite. In these, the sodium atoms are inserted between the layers of carbon atoms in the graphite.

Sodium also reacts with liquid ammonia to form sodium amide ($NaNH_2$). It forms two compounds with nitrogen—sodium nitride (Na_3N) and sodium azide (NaN_3). At room temperature, the reaction of sodium with nitrogen is extremely slow. This is why sodium metal is often stored in nitrogen.

ATOMS AT WORK

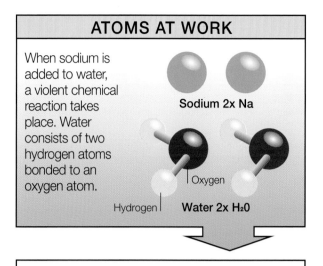

When sodium is added to water, a violent chemical reaction takes place. Water consists of two hydrogen atoms bonded to an oxygen atom.

Sodium 2x Na

Oxygen

Hydrogen

Water 2x H_2O

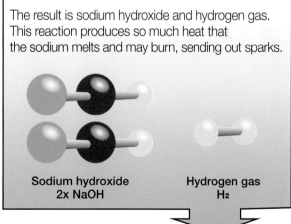

The bonds holding together the water molecules break, and the atoms can recombine in new ways.

Oxygen

Hydrogen

Sodium

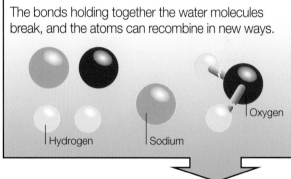

The result is sodium hydroxide and hydrogen gas. This reaction produces so much heat that the sodium melts and may burn, sending out sparks.

Sodium hydroxide
2x NaOH

Hydrogen gas
H_2

The reaction can be written like this:

2Na + 2H_2O → 2NaOH + H_2

The number of atoms of each element is the same on both sides of the reaction.

An energetic reaction takes place when a pellet of sodium metal is dropped onto water. The sodium reacts with the water to make a solution of sodium hydroxide (NaOH). The sodium fizzes as hydrogen gas is released by the reaction.

Sodium compounds

The most familiar sodium compound is salt. You have it in your salt shaker, and you can taste it in the sea and in the sweat your body produces to cool down. Salt seems so common, we hardly think about using it. In ancient times, however, salt was so valuable that it was used as money and wars were fought over it.

To chemists, salt is known as sodium chloride. It is an ionic compound with a melting point of 1,472°F (800°C). Within a piece of salt, the ions are

Salt has been a very valuable substance throughout history. This medieval painting shows a man buying goods, using salt as a form of money.

arranged in a structure called a crystal lattice, in which each sodium ion is surrounded by six chlorine ions, and each chlorine ion is surrounded by six sodium ions. When salt is dissolved in water, the ions are pulled apart and can move around.

Salt has many uses. We use it in cooking to improve the flavor of food. Before refrigerators were invented, meat and fish were preserved in salt to make them last longer. Salt is still used as a preservative in the canning industry. Salt lowers the freezing point of water, so it is sprinkled on icy roads and sidewalks to melt the ice.

Sodium chloride is also a starting point for other useful products. There are large amounts of salt around the world, and it is easy to extract and cheap to produce.

Sea salt is produced when seawater in shallow salt pans evaporates in the sun. The large crystals of sodium chloride are then scooped into mounds to dry.

Getting salt

Most salt is mined from deep underground deposits. A shaft is dug to reach the salt bed, and the salt is blasted out of the rock using explosives. Then, once it has been brought to the surface, the salt is crushed. Some salt is produced by solution mining. In this method, water is pumped into the underground deposit. The sodium chloride dissolves and the solution (called brine) is pumped to the surface. When the brine reaches the surface, it is put in special vacuum flasks, which evaporate the water and leave the salt crystals behind.

The oldest source of salt is the sea, and evaporation of seawater is still used to get salt today. People build shallow salt pans,

---

DID YOU KNOW?

SALT FROM SPACE

On March 22, 1998, a meteorite fell to Earth in west Texas. A group of boys found the meteorite and took it to the Johnson Space Center in Houston. Scientists at the center split the meteorite open and found salt crystals inside. The crystals were dated at 4.5 billion years old—almost as old as our Sun and our Solar System.

Halite is dug out of underground shafts using huge cutting machines. The salt beds are about 980 feet (300 meters) below Earth's surface.

which fill with seawater. The Sun heats the water, and a very concentrated brine solution forms. Eventually, crystals of sodium chloride settle at the bottom of the pans, and the rest of the solution is drained off. This produces a very coarse form of salt with large crystals called sea salt.

Sodium carbonate

Sodium carbonate was originally made from plants. The plants were burned, and the sodium carbonate was extracted from the ashes. This gave the compound the name soda ash. However, large numbers of plants were needed for this process, and it produced very little sodium carbonate.

The first industrial process for making sodium carbonate was invented in 1789 by French chemist Nicolas Leblanc (1742–1806). He mixed sodium chloride with sulfuric acid, limestone rock, and charcoal. In 1861, Belgian chemist Ernest Solvay (1838–1922) invented an easier way of making sodium carbonate. In the Solvay process—which is still used today—ammonia and carbon dioxide are bubbled through a strong solution of brine. The reaction produces ammonium hydrogen carbonate. This compound reacts with sodium chloride to make ammonium

In an industrial furnace, sodium carbonate is combined with calcium oxide and silicon dioxide to make molten glass, which is then formed into sheets.

SODIUM BICARBONATE FACTS

⬤ Sodium bicarbonate is used in antacids to help relieve indigestion. Because sodium bicarbonate is mildly alkaline, it neutralizes excess hydrochloric acid in the stomach. It also provides the fizz you see when you dissolve an antacid tablet in a glass of water.

⬤ Beestings are slightly acidic. Rubbing a paste of baking soda and water onto a beesting neutralizes the sting and relieves the pain.

⬤ Sodium bicarbonate is used inside dry-chemical fire extinguishers. When a lever is pressed, these give off carbon dioxide gas, which smothers fires and puts them out.

ATOMS AT WORK

The final stage of the Solvay process changes sodium bicarbonate into sodium carbonate. When sodium bicarbonate is heated, the heat supplies energy that breaks the bonds holding the molecule together.

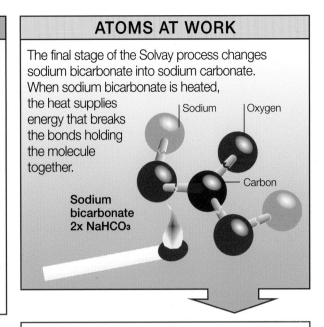

Sodium bicarbonate
2x $NaHCO_3$

The result is sodium carbonate, water, and carbon dioxide gas.

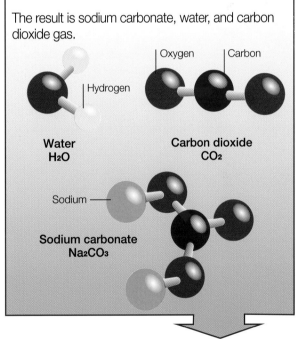

Water
H_2O

Carbon dioxide
CO_2

Sodium carbonate
Na_2CO_3

The reaction that takes place when sodium bicarbonate is heated is written like this:

$$2NaHCO_3 \rightarrow Na_2CO_3 + H_2O + CO_2$$

Nothing has been added or removed from the reaction, but the atoms have joined up in new ways to make new compounds.

chloride solution and crystals of sodium bicarbonate. The sodium bicarbonate is heated to give sodium carbonate.

Sodium carbonate is a very important industrial chemical. Several million tons of it are used each year. About a third is used to make glass, and the rest is used to treat sewage, to soften water, and to make paper, chemicals, and detergents. Hydrated sodium carbonate is better known as washing soda and is used as bath salts and as a water softener.

Sodium bicarbonate

Sodium bicarbonate, or sodium hydrogen carbonate, is also a useful compound. Often called baking soda, this sodium compound is the main ingredient of baking powder. Baking powder is a mixture of an acid (usually cream

Sodium compounds are used in many ways you might not expect. Here, scientists are using sodium bicarbonate very carefully to clean dirt from a dinosaur bone without damaging it.

SEE FOR YOURSELF

PRODUCING CARBON DIOXIDE

You can see how baking powder works by stirring it into a glass of hot water. You should see plenty of bubbles! For an even more explosive reaction, you can add baking soda to a dilute acid. Put some baking soda in a container and pour vinegar on it (ask an adult to help). Stand back and watch what happens! You should hear fizzing and crackling as the sodium bicarbonate in the baking soda reacts with the vinegar (an acid) to release carbon dioxide gas.

of tartar, or potassium acid tartrate) with a base (sodium bicarbonate). When baking powder is added to a wet cake mixture it dissolves. The acid reacts with the sodium bicarbonate to produce carbon dioxide gas, which bubbles into the mixture and makes the cake rise.

Single-acting baking powder produces carbon dioxide when it gets wet. Double-acting baking powder gets its name because it produces bubbles again when it is heated above 122°F (50°C). Some recipes call for baking soda rather than baking powder. In these recipes, the acid is usually provided by another ingredient, such as yogurt, buttermilk, honey, molasses, lemon juice, or orange juice.

Sodium hydroxide

Sodium hydroxide, also known as lye, is a white solid with a melting point of 604°F (318°C). Sodium hydroxide crystals absorb water very easily and will soak up moisture from the air. When they are dissolved in water, they make a strongly alkaline solution. Both the solid and the solution must be handled with great care. Solid sodium hydroxide burns the skin, and this has given it another name—caustic soda. It also dissolves fat and grease, so it is often poured down household drains to unblock them. Close proximity to or ingestion of this solution can cause blindness, permanent scarring, and even death.

In industry, sodium hydroxide solution is used to make cellophane, rayon, bleaches, dyes, and drugs. It is used in the petrochemical industry to remove impurities, such as hydrogen sulfide from petroleum. If hydrogen sulfide is left in petroleum, it causes pollution and leads to acid rain. In the paper industry, sodium hydroxide breaks down lignin in wood. Lignin is the glue that holds cellulose fibers together. When the lignin is removed, the fibers can be turned into paper.

Making soap

People have been making soap since the twelfth century by boiling fats with alkalis. Today, the fat is a long-chain organic compound called stearic acid, and

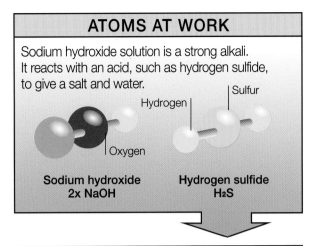

ATOMS AT WORK

Sodium hydroxide solution is a strong alkali. It reacts with an acid, such as hydrogen sulfide, to give a salt and water.

Hydrogen

Sulfur

Oxygen

Sodium hydroxide
2x NaOH

Hydrogen sulfide
H₂S

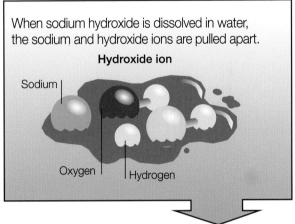

When sodium hydroxide is dissolved in water, the sodium and hydroxide ions are pulled apart.

Hydroxide ion

Sodium

Oxygen

Hydrogen

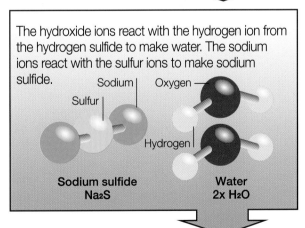

The hydroxide ions react with the hydrogen ion from the hydrogen sulfide to make water. The sodium ions react with the sulfur ions to make sodium sulfide.

Sodium

Oxygen

Sulfur

Hydrogen

Sodium sulfide
Na₂S

Water
2x H₂O

The reaction that takes place can be written like this:

2NaOH + H₂S → Na₂S + H₂O

The atoms have joined up in different combinations to make new compounds.

Sodium hydroxide is used in paper making to break down the lignin in wood. In this picture, wood pulp is being spread onto a moving belt at a paper mill.

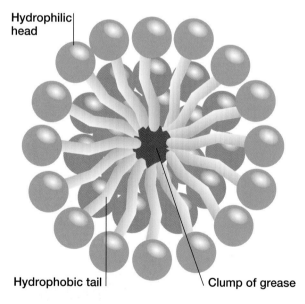

The hydrophilic heads around the outside of this ball of sodium stearate molecules are attracted to water and can be rinsed away. The grease is attached to the hydrophobic tails and is washed away, too.

the alkali is sodium hydroxide. When these are heated together, the sodium replaces a hydrogen atom to make a long-chain organic salt called sodium stearate. Soap is largely sodium stearate with perfumes and colors added to make the soap smell nice and look more attractive.

Sodium stearate molecules have a water-hating (hydrophobic) end and a water-loving (hydrophilic) end. The soap molecules surround a clump of dirt or grease. The water-hating ends dig deep into the dirt, surrounding it with a ring of sodium stearate molecules. The water-loving ends are attracted to water, so the clumps of dirt can be rinsed away.

Hard water

If you have ever washed your hands with soap and been unable to make a lather, you were probably in an area where the water is "hard." Hard water has calcium and magnesium salts dissolved in it. They react with soap (sodium stearate) to make calcium and magnesium stearates. These compounds do not dissolve in water, and they float to the surface as a dirty "scum."

Sodium nitrate acts as an oxidizing agent in dynamite. This means that it causes other chemicals to react with oxygen, making the explosive stronger.

COMPOUND FACTS

There are many different sodium compounds. Here are just some of the sodium compounds you might come across:

⊙ sodium nitrate (Chile saltpeter)—used as a fertilizer and to make dynamite

⊙ sodium sulfate—used to make glass and detergents

⊙ sodium hypochlorite—used to make bleach

⊙ sodium thiosulfite—used as a lubricant and a drying agent

⊙ sodium arsenate—used as a pesticide

⊙ sodium aluminum fluoride—used as a supply of aluminum

⊙ sodium sulfite—used as a food additive to prevent the growth of microorganisms.

How sodium is used

As you walk along a street on dark winter evenings, the soft orange glow of the streetlamps lights your way. Streetlamps are filled with sodium vapor. When an electrical current is passed through the vapor, the sodium glows with a yellow-orange light.

In the past, large quantities of sodium were used to make tetraethyl lead. This compound was added to gasoline to prevent the gasoline igniting at the wrong time. The ignition made a loud knocking, and so tetraethyl lead is also called antiknock. However, gasolines that contain lead produce harmful gases in their exhaust fumes, and many people are worried that the waste products from this compound cause lead poisoning and pollute the environment. As a result, leaded gas is being phased out in many countries.

Because it is so reactive, sodium can be used to extract other metals from their ores in a process called refining. The sodium replaces the other metals in their compounds. It is used in the preparation of calcium, zirconium, and titanium. Sodium is also used as a catalyst in industrial processes and as a starting point to make sodium hydride and sodium peroxide.

Sodium is very good at conducting heat and is used in cooling chambers (shown below) in nuclear power stations. A mixture of sodium and potassium is used to carry heat away from the nuclear reactor to heat exchangers, where the heat is turned into electricity.

Sodium in living things

Sodium ions are found in the body fluids of all animals. These fluids include sweat, plasma (the liquid part of blood), and the fluid that bathes all the cells of the body. Sodium is important in sending nerve impulses and in homeostasis— the way the body keeps its conditions constant. Both of these are essential for living things to interact with their environment and to remain healthy.

Sending messages

When you turn the pages of this book, messages from your brain pass through your body to the muscles in your hand and make them move. The signals pass through the nervous system, which is made up of millions of nerve cells. The messages that pass to and from the brain telling us what to do are sent by tiny electrical impulses that move from one nerve cell to the next. These electrical impulses are created by the movement of sodium ions into and out of cells in the body.

Sodium and potassium ions are found in all animal cells. There are usually more potassium ions inside the cell and more sodium ions in the fluid around the cells. When a nerve cell is triggered, sodium ions rush into the cell and potassium moves out. This changes the concentration

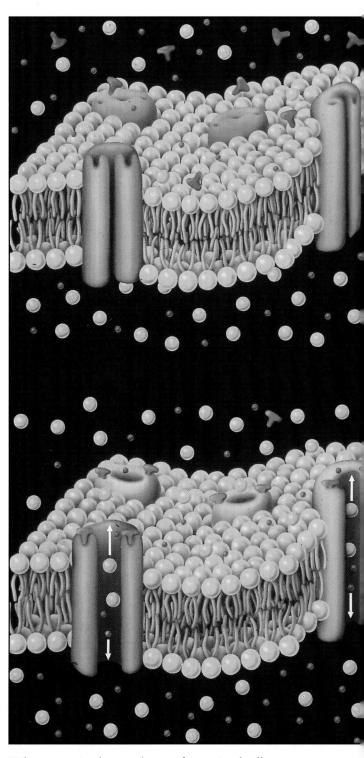

When pores in the membrane of an animal cell open (below), sodium ions (the red balls) pass into the cell, and potassium ions (the blue balls) move out.

of sodium and potassium ions and creates an electrical pulse. The electrical pulse travels down a part of the cell called the axon until it reaches a synapse (a contact

Sharks have a gland near their rectum that produces a concentrated salt solution. These animals also have an osmotic pressure similar to that of seawater because they keep nitrogen-containing waste products in their body tissues.

with another nerve cell or a muscle fiber). There, the signal triggers the release of chemicals that stimulate another electrical impulse or a contraction in the other cell.

Homeostasis

Body fluids contain dissolved sodium and chlorine ions—in other words, a solution of salt. The dissolved ions give body fluids what is known as an osmotic pressure, which is important for animal cells to work properly. The concentration of sodium ions regulates the amount of water the cells contain and also helps the body stay at a constant pH (a measure of how acid or alkaline something is). This is important, because enzymes—the substances that

---

DID YOU KNOW?

ELIMINATING SALT

Animals that live in salty places build up high levels of salt in their body, which they need to remove to keep their osmotic pressure constant. Most marine fish have special cells in their gills that get rid of sodium chloride. Some marine and desert birds get rid of salt through special glands near their eyes that produce very salty tears.

Saltwater plants have the same problem in regulating their osmotic pressure as marine animals do. Mangrove trees, for example, grow in coastal waters. Some species have roots that can filter out salt, while others have glands in their leaves that can get rid of it.

---

allow life-sustaining reactions to take place—work best at certain pH levels. Sweat is salty, as you know from its taste. The body produces sweat when it is hot. The sweat evaporates, and the body cools. This is another example of homeostasis—we sweat when we are hot to stop our body heating up.

In vertebrates (animals with a backbone), the amount of salt and water in the body is regulated by the kidneys.

SODIUM FACTS

SODIUM IN FOOD

	Amount	Milligrams sodium
Table salt	1 teaspoon	2,132
Soy sauce	1 tablespoon	920
Tomato juice	6 ounces (170 g)	658
Pretzels	1 ounce (28.4 g)	486
Peas, canned	½ cup	277
Potato chips	1 ounce (28.4 g)	168

chips, pretzels, and pickles are also very high in salt. Too much salt leads to high blood pressure, which can cause heart problems. Many people are cutting down on the amount of salt they eat or are using low-sodium alternatives in its place.

These organs filter waste from the body, absorbing useful products such as salt and excreting the rest as urine.

Salt in the diet

Our body contains about 3.5 ounces (100 grams) of salt. Some of this is lost each day through our skin or in our urine, so it has to be replaced. Lack of salt causes weakness, dizziness, headaches, and muscle cramps. However, this lack of salt is rarely caused by a poor diet. All the salt we need can be got from normal foodstuffs.

On average, a person eats about 0.3 ounces (10 grams) of salt a day, although only 1–2 grams of salt are actually needed. Sources of salt include table salt, soy sauce, monosodium glutamate, cheese, smoked meats, and processed and canned goods—many of the foods we eat already contain more than enough salt before we add it in cooking or at the table. Snack foods such as potato

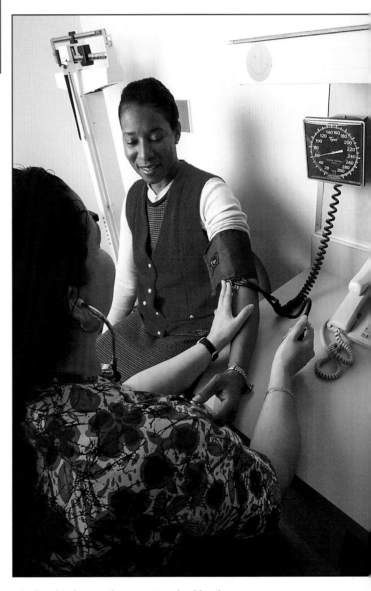

A diet high in salt can raise the blood pressure. This doctor is checking her patient's blood pressure using an instrument called a sphygmomanometer.

Periodic table

Everything in the Universe is made from combinations of substances called elements. Elements are the building blocks of matter. They are made of tiny atoms, which are much too small to see.

The character of an atom depends on how many even tinier particles called protons there are in its center, or nucleus. An element's atomic number is the same as the number of protons.

Scientists have found more than 110 different elements. About 90 elements occur naturally on Earth. The rest have been made in experiments.

All these elements are set out on a chart called the periodic table. This lists all the elements in order according to their atomic number.

The elements at the left of the table are metals. Those at the right are nonmetals. Between the metals and the nonmetals are the metalloids, which sometimes act like metals and sometimes like nonmetals.

- On the left of the table are the alkali metals. These elements have just one electron in their outer shells.

- Elements get more reactive as you go down a group.

- On the right of the periodic table are the noble gases. These elements have full outer shells.

- The number of electrons orbiting the nucleus increases down each group.

- Elements in the same group have the same number of electrons in their outer shells.

- The transition metals are in the middle of the table, between Groups II and III.

Group I

Group II

Transition metals

1 **H** Hydrogen 1								
3 **Li** Lithium 7	4 **Be** Beryllium 9							
11 **Na** Sodium 23	12 **Mg** Magnesium 24							
19 **K** Potassium 39	20 **Ca** Calcium 40	21 **Sc** Scandium 45	22 **Ti** Titanium 48	23 **V** Vanadium 51	24 **Cr** Chromium 52	25 **Mn** Manganese 55	26 **Fe** Iron 56	27 **Co** Cobalt 59
37 **Rb** Rubidium 85	38 **Sr** Strontium 88	39 **Y** Yttrium 89	40 **Zr** Zirconium 91	41 **Nb** Niobium 93	42 **Mo** Molybdenum 96	43 **Tc** Technetium (98)	44 **Ru** Ruthenium 101	45 **Rh** Rhodium 103
55 **Cs** Cesium 133	56 **Ba** Barium 137	71 **Lu** Lutetium 175	72 **Hf** Hafnium 179	73 **Ta** Tantalum 181	74 **W** Tungsten 184	75 **Re** Rhenium 186	76 **Os** Osmium 190	77 **Ir** Iridium 192
87 **Fr** Francium 223	88 **Ra** Radium 226	103 **Lr** Lawrencium (260)	104 **Unq** Unnilquadium (261)	105 **Unp** Unnilpentium (262)	106 **Unh** Unnilhexium (263)	107 **Uns** Unnilseptium (?)	108 **Uno** Unniloctium (?)	109 **Une** Unillenium (?)

Lanthanide elements

Actinide elements

57 **La** Lanthanum 39	58 **Ce** Cerium 140	59 **Pr** Praseodymium 141	60 **Nd** Neodymium 144	61 **Pm** Promethium (145)
89 **Ac** Actinium 227	90 **Th** Thorium 232	91 **Pa** Protactinium 231	92 **U** Uranium 238	93 **Np** Neptunium (237)

The horizontal rows are called periods. As you go across a period, the atomic number increases by one from each element to the next. The vertical columns are called groups. Elements get heavier as you go down a group. All the elements in a group have the same number of electrons in their outer shells. This means they react in similar ways.

The transition metals fall between Groups II and III. Their electron shells fill up in an unusual way. The lanthanide elements and the actinide elements are set apart from the main table to make it easier to read. All the lanthanide elements and the actinide elements are quite rare.

Sodium in the table

Sodium has atomic number 11, so it has 11 protons in its nucleus. It lies in Group I with lithium, potassium, rubidium, cesium, and francium. All these elements have a single electron in their outer electron shell. This group is also called the alkali metals, because they react with water to form alkalis (substances that neutralize acids).

Legend:
- Metals
- Metalloids (semimetals)
- Nonmetals

Key box:
- 11 — Atomic (proton) number
- Na — Symbol
- Sodium — Name
- 23 — Atomic mass

			Group III	Group IV	Group V	Group VI	Group VII	Group VIII
								2 He Helium 4
			5 B Boron 11	6 C Carbon 12	7 N Nitrogen 14	8 O Oxygen 16	9 F Fluorine 19	10 Ne Neon 20
			13 Al Aluminum 27	14 Si Silicon 28	15 P Phosphorus 31	16 S Sulfur 32	17 Cl Chlorine 35	18 Ar Argon 40
28 Ni Nickel 59	29 Cu Copper 64	30 Zn Zinc 65	31 Ga Gallium 70	32 Ge Germanium 73	33 As Arsenic 75	34 Se Selenium 79	35 Br Bromine 80	36 Kr Krypton 84
46 Pd Palladium 106	47 Ag Silver 108	48 Cd Cadmium 112	49 In Indium 115	50 Sn Tin 119	51 Sb Antimony 122	52 Te Tellurium 128	53 I Iodine 127	54 Xe Xenon 131
78 Pt Platinum 195	79 Au Gold 197	80 Hg Mercury 201	81 Tl Thallium 204	82 Pb Lead 207	83 Bi Bismuth 209	84 Po Polonium (209)	85 At Astatine (210)	86 Rn Radon (222)

62 Sm Samarium 150	63 Eu Europium 152	64 Gd Gadolinium 157	65 Tb Terbium 159	66 Dy Dysprosium 163	67 Ho Holmium 165	68 Er Erbium 167	69 Tm Thulium 169	70 Yb Ytterbium 173
94 Pu Plutonium (244)	95 Am Americium (243)	96 Cm Curium (247)	97 Bk Berkelium (247)	98 Cf Californium (251)	99 Es Einsteinium (252)	100 Fm Fermium (257)	101 Md Mendelevium (258)	102 No Nobelium (259)

Chemical reactions

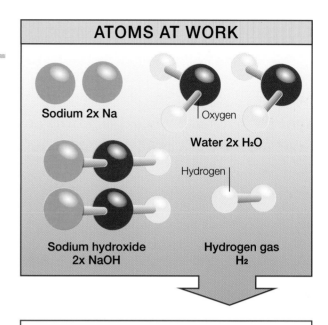

ATOMS AT WORK

Sodium 2x Na

Oxygen

Water 2x H₂O

Hydrogen

Sodium hydroxide
2x NaOH

Hydrogen gas
H₂

Chemical reactions are going on all the time—candles burn, nails rust, food is digested. Some reactions involve just two substances; others many more. But whenever a reaction takes place, at least one substance is changed.

In a chemical reaction, the atoms stay the same. But they join up in different combinations to form new molecules.

Writing an equation

Chemical reactions can be described by writing down the atoms and molecules before and the atoms and molecules after. Since the atoms stay the same, the number of atoms before will be the same

The reaction that takes place when sodium reacts with water can be written like this:

$$2Na + 2H_2O \rightarrow 2NaOH + H_2$$

The number of atoms of each element is the same on both sides of the reaction, but new compounds have formed as the atoms joined up in new ways.

as the number of atoms after. Chemists write the reaction as an equation. The equation shows what happens in the chemical reaction.

When the numbers of each atom on both sides of the equation are equal, the equation is balanced. If the numbers are not equal, something is wrong. The chemist adjusts the number of atoms involved until the equation does balance.

This woman is making soap from lye, or sodium hydroxide. The sodium hydroxide reacts with stearic acid to make sodium stearate molecules in the soap.

Glossary

atom: The smallest part of an element that has all the properties of that element.

atomic mass: The number of protons and neutrons in an atom.

atomic number: The number of protons in an atom.

Big Bang: The huge explosion in space that some scientists believe occurred when the Universe began.

bond: The attraction between two atoms that holds them together.

catalyst: Something that makes a chemical reaction occur more quickly.

compound: A substance that is made of atoms of more than one element. The atoms in a compound are held together by chemical bonds.

crystal: A solid substance in which the atoms are arranged in a regular three-dimensional pattern.

electrolysis: The use of electricity to change a substance chemically.

electrolyte: A liquid that electricity can flow through.

electron: A tiny particle with a negative charge. Electrons are found inside atoms, where they move around the nucleus in layers called electron shells.

element: A substance that is made from only one type of atom. Sodium is one of the metallic elements.

evaporation: A process in which liquid turns to vapor. Evaporation takes place at a temperature below boiling point.

halite: A mineral form of sodium chloride.

ion: A particle that is similar to an atom but carries an additional negative or positive electrical charge.

metal: An element on the left-hand side of the periodic table.

meteorite: A piece of rock that fell to Earth from space.

neutron: A tiny particle with no electrical charge. It is found in the nucleus of almost every atom.

nonmetal: An element on the right-hand side of the periodic table.

nucleus: The center of an atom. It contains protons and neutrons.

ore: A collection of minerals from which metals, in particular, are usually extracted.

oxidation: A reaction where oxygen is added to, or one or more electrons are removed from, a substance.

periodic table: A chart of all the chemical elements laid out in order of their atomic number.

proton: A tiny particle with a positive charge. Protons are found inside the nucleus of an atom.

refining: An industrial process that frees elements, such as metals, from impurities or unwanted material.

solvent: A liquid that can dissolve one or more other substances.

Index

12/02

ML